The Eternal Loop

The Eternal Loop

Matthew Petchinsky

The Eternal Loop: Finding Purpose in Repetition
By: Matthew Petchinsky

Introduction: Insights from *Groundhog Day* and Its Themes

The 1993 film *Groundhog Day*, directed by Harold Ramis and starring Bill Murray as Phil Connors, is more than a charming romantic comedy; it is a profound exploration of human existence, personal transformation, and the quest for meaning. The movie's premise is deceptively simple yet deeply philosophical: Phil, a cynical and self-absorbed weatherman, finds himself inexplicably reliving the same day—Groundhog Day—in Punxsutawney, Pennsylvania, over and over again. What begins as a humorous premise soon evolves into a narrative filled with existential depth, moral exploration, and spiritual enlightenment.

This introduction aims to delve into the many layers of meaning that *Groundhog Day* offers, highlighting its universal appeal and its enduring relevance. The film has been interpreted as a commentary on human behavior, spiritual awakening, and the cyclical nature of life. It speaks to our struggles with monotony, our desire for change, and our ultimate realization that true happiness often lies within ourselves. In examining these themes, we uncover why *Groundhog Day* resonates so profoundly with audiences across cultures and generations.

A Mirror to Our Lives: The Monotony of Routine

One of the most relatable aspects of *Groundhog Day* is its portrayal of monotony—a sentiment experienced by nearly everyone at some point in life. Phil Connors' predicament mirrors the drudgery of a repetitive existence where days blend together, and life feels stagnant. Many viewers see themselves in Phil as he initially reacts to his situation with frustration, boredom, and reckless abandon, echoing the way people cope with the monotony of daily routines.

This theme challenges us to reflect on how we approach our own lives when faced with seemingly unchanging circumstances. Are we merely going through the motions, or can we find opportunities for growth even in repetition? *Groundhog Day* suggests that the way out of monotony lies not in changing external circumstances but in transforming our internal perspective.

The Journey of Transformation: From Selfishness to Selflessness

Phil's evolution throughout the film forms the heart of its narrative. At the outset, he embodies selfishness, arrogance, and apathy. He views others as tools to serve his needs or as obstacles to his desires. However, as the day continues to repeat, he begins to recognize the futility of his self-centered ways and embarks on a journey of self-improvement and connection.

This transformation is deeply resonant because it reflects the human potential for growth and redemption. Through his experiences, Phil learns to genuinely care for others, mastering the art of selflessness. He saves lives, offers kindness, and becomes an active participant in his community. This evolution underscores the idea that fulfillment comes not from taking but from giving—a lesson that transcends cultures and time.

Redemption Through Mastery: The Pursuit of Excellence

As Phil's journey unfolds, he takes advantage of his seemingly infinite time loop to cultivate new skills and passions. He learns to play the piano, sculpt ice, and develop a deeper understanding of those around him. This aspect of the film highlights the value of personal mastery as a path to self-actualization.

The concept of mastery serves as a metaphor for the idea that life's repetitions—our mistakes, setbacks, and trials—can become opportunities to refine ourselves. Instead of succumbing to despair, Phil uses his time to become a better version of himself, showcasing the transformative power of dedication and persistence.

The Spiritual Dimension: Groundhog Day as an Allegory

Many interpretations of *Groundhog Day* view it as a spiritual allegory, exploring themes of karma, enlightenment, and the cycles of existence. Phil's journey through the time loop mirrors the Buddhist concept of samsara—the endless cycle of birth, death, and rebirth—until one attains enlightenment. In this context, the film suggests that breaking free from this cycle requires inner awakening and the transcendence of selfish desires.

Similarly, the movie resonates with Christian themes of redemption and grace. Phil's transformation from a sinner consumed by greed and lust to a virtuous individual who embraces love and selflessness mirrors the spiritual journey of repentance and renewal. This spiritual undertone lends the film a timeless quality, allowing viewers to interpret its messages through their own faiths and philosophies.

The Role of Love and Connection

At its core, *Groundhog Day* is also a love story—one that goes beyond romantic love. While Phil's relationship with his producer, Rita (played by Andie MacDowell), is a central thread, the film emphasizes the broader concept of love: love for others, for life, and for oneself. Through Rita's kindness and patience, Phil begins to see a better version of himself reflected back to him, inspiring his transformation.

The film suggests that true love is not about manipulation or self-serving goals but about understanding, empathy, and mutual respect. This theme reinforces the idea that human connection is essential to finding meaning and breaking free from isolation.

A Universal Message: The Power of Choice

Ultimately, *Groundhog Day* is a meditation on the power of choice. While Phil cannot control the time loop, he learns that he can control his actions and reactions within it. This realization empowers him to live each day as if it matters—a lesson that resonates universally.

The film's message is clear: even in the face of circumstances we cannot change, we have the power to shape our responses, find meaning, and create joy. It reminds us that life's value lies not in its length but in its depth, and that each moment offers an opportunity to grow, connect, and make a difference.

In conclusion, *Groundhog Day* is far more than a quirky romantic comedy. It is a profound exploration of life's deepest questions: How do we find meaning in monotony? How can we transform ourselves? What role do love and connection play in our journey? By examining these themes, the film invites us to reflect on our own lives and inspires us to approach each day with gratitude, purpose, and an open heart. Its lessons are timeless, offering wisdom and comfort to anyone seeking to navigate the complexities of existence.

Chapter 1: The Allure of Repetition in Everyday Life

Repetition is a paradoxical force in human existence. On the one hand, it provides stability, predictability, and comfort, anchoring us in familiar routines. On the other hand, it can feel stifling, mundane, and monotonous, leading to a sense of entrapment or boredom. In *Groundhog Day*, Phil Connors' time loop encapsulates this paradox. While initially horrifying and frustrating, the repetition becomes the crucible for his personal growth and self-realization. To understand how repetition shapes our lives, we must first explore why it is so alluring—and at times, so oppressive.

The Comfort of Routine: Why We Gravitate Toward Repetition

Humans are creatures of habit. From the moment we wake up to the time we go to bed, our lives are often governed by routines. Morning coffee, the daily commute, and the evening wind-down are rituals that provide a sense of structure. This predictability has evolutionary roots. In an unpredictable and often dangerous world, routines have historically ensured survival by conserving mental energy for critical decisions.

In modern life, repetition continues to serve as a psychological anchor. It reduces decision fatigue, allowing us to focus our cognitive resources on more significant tasks. For example, following a morning routine frees us from the mental burden of deciding anew how to start each day. Repetition offers a sense of control in an uncontrollable world, creating a comforting rhythm in the face of chaos.

The Other Side of the Coin: The Monotony of Repetition

However, what provides stability can also lead to stagnation. The very routines that ground us can become shackles, limiting our experiences and growth. In *Groundhog Day*, Phil Connors initially sees his repetitive existence as a prison. His frustration mirrors the universal human experience of feeling trapped in the grind of daily life. The monotony of repetition can drain our energy, leaving us yearning for novelty and change.

This duality—comfort versus monotony—is at the heart of the allure and danger of repetition. Too much routine, and life begins to feel like an endless loop. Too little, and we face the anxiety of unpredictability. Striking a balance is crucial, but as Phil's journey shows, finding this balance often requires introspection and intentional action.

The Allure of Mastery: Repetition as a Tool for Growth

Repetition also holds a hidden potential: the path to mastery. Whether it's learning to play an instrument, mastering a craft, or developing a skill, repetition is the cornerstone of improvement. In *Groundhog Day*, Phil's eventual embrace of repetition allows him to cultivate talents like piano playing and ice sculpting. His journey demonstrates that when approached with the right mindset, repetition can be transformative.

The concept of "deliberate practice" underscores this idea. Psychologist Anders Ericsson's research on expertise reveals that repetitive, intentional practice is the key to becoming proficient in any field. Repetition, when coupled with a desire to improve, transforms from a burden into a powerful tool for self-actualization.

The Psychological Need for Novelty and Routine

Why do we crave both repetition and novelty? Psychologists suggest that humans have a dual need for stability and exploration. Routine provides the safety of the known, while novelty offers the excitement of the unknown. The tension between these needs drives much of human behavior.

Phil Connors' journey reflects this tension. Initially, his repetitive existence is devoid of novelty, leading to despair. As he learns to introduce new elements—like helping others, developing skills, and fostering connections—he strikes a balance between the stability of repetition and the excitement of growth. This balance is key to finding fulfillment in a repetitive world.

Breaking the Cycle: Repetition as a Catalyst for Change

Repetition, paradoxically, can be the very thing that forces us to change. When life becomes repetitive, we are confronted with ourselves in ways we cannot escape. In *Groundhog Day*, Phil is forced to face his flaws, desires, and limitations because of the unrelenting sameness of his existence. The time loop becomes a mirror, reflecting his actions and compelling him to evolve.

In everyday life, repetitive experiences often highlight patterns in our behavior. For example, repeatedly encountering similar challenges at work or in relationships may reveal areas where we need to grow. By examining these patterns, we can use repetition as a catalyst for transformation, just as Phil does.

The Spiritual Perspective: Repetition as a Path to Enlightenment

In many spiritual traditions, repetition is a tool for achieving enlightenment or transcendence. Practices like meditation, chanting, and prayer involve repetitive actions that quiet the mind and foster self-awareness. These practices suggest that repetition, far from being mundane, can be sacred.

Phil's journey in *Groundhog Day* mirrors this spiritual perspective. His repeated experiences force him to look inward, shed his ego, and embrace selflessness. In this way, the time loop becomes not a punishment but a path to spiritual awakening—a theme that resonates deeply with audiences from diverse backgrounds.

Applying the Lessons of Repetition to Everyday Life

What can we learn from *Groundhog Day* about the role of repetition in our own lives? First, it reminds us to examine our routines and assess whether they are serving us or holding us back. Are our habits leading to growth, or are they keeping us stagnant? Second, it encourages us to view repetition not as a trap but as an opportunity. Each day, no matter how similar to the last, offers a chance to improve, connect, and find meaning.

Finally, the film teaches us to balance routine with novelty. By incorporating small changes into our daily lives—trying a new hobby, reaching out to someone we care about, or simply taking a different route to work—we can break the monotony without sacrificing the comfort of stability.

In conclusion, repetition is a powerful force in human life, offering both comfort and challenge. As *Groundhog Day* illustrates, how we approach repetition determines whether it becomes a source of despair or a path to fulfillment. By embracing the transformative potential of repetition, we can find meaning in even the most mundane aspects of our existence and unlock our capacity for growth and self-discovery.

Chapter 2: Lessons from Phil: Growth Through Routine

Phil Connors, the protagonist of *Groundhog Day*, embarks on a journey of profound personal transformation, catalyzed by an endless repetition of the same day. While his predicament is unique—a fantastical time loop trapping him in Punxsutawney—it mirrors the everyday cycles of life that we all experience. Phil's evolution from a selfish, cynical man to a compassionate, self-aware individual offers valuable lessons about how routine, often perceived as mundane, can become a powerful tool for growth.

The Initial Resistance: The Struggle Against Repetition

At the start of the film, Phil's response to the time loop is one of frustration, disbelief, and rebellion. Like many of us, he resists the monotony of routine, viewing it as a trap that limits his freedom and potential. This initial resistance is a natural human reaction to repetitive circumstances. We often feel confined by the patterns of daily life, yearning for change and novelty.

Phil's struggle reflects a universal truth: before growth can occur, we must confront and accept the reality of our circumstances. His early attempts to break free—through reckless indulgence, manipulation, and even despair—demonstrate the futility of fighting against the inevitable. It is only when he begins to embrace the repetition that his journey of growth truly begins.

The Turning Point: Acceptance and Self-Reflection

Phil's transformation begins with a crucial shift: acceptance. Instead of resisting the time loop, he starts to reflect on his behavior and its impact on others. This turning point is significant because it marks the moment when routine becomes a mirror, forcing him to confront his flaws and limitations.

In our own lives, routines can serve a similar purpose. The predictability of daily patterns creates opportunities for self-reflection and self-improvement. By examining our habits and behaviors within the context of routine, we can identify areas for growth and begin the process of transformation.

Embracing the Routine: Repetition as a Playground for Growth

Once Phil accepts the time loop, he begins to see it not as a prison but as a playground—a space where he can experiment, learn, and grow without fear of long-term consequences. He starts to cultivate new skills, such as piano playing and ice sculpting, and to deepen his understanding of the people around him.

This shift highlights an important lesson: routine, when approached with curiosity and intention, can be a fertile ground for growth. Instead of viewing repetition as monotonous, we can use it as an opportunity to refine our skills, explore new interests, and build meaningful connections.

Developing Emotional Intelligence: Learning to Truly See Others

One of Phil's most significant lessons comes through his interactions with the people of Punxsutawney. At the start of the film, he views them as caricatures—background players in the story of his life. However, as he relives the day repeatedly, he begins to see them as individuals with their own struggles, dreams, and humanity.

This growth in emotional intelligence is a key aspect of Phil's transformation. By taking the time to understand and empathize with others, he becomes more compassionate and connected. This lesson underscores the importance of using routine interactions—whether with coworkers, family members, or strangers—as opportunities to practice empathy and build deeper relationships.

Mastery Through Repetition: The Power of Deliberate Practice

Phil's journey demonstrates the transformative power of deliberate practice. By engaging with the same day repeatedly, he is able to hone his skills and achieve mastery in various areas. This aspect of the film aligns with psychological research on skill development, which emphasizes the importance of consistent, focused practice in achieving expertise.

In our own lives, routines provide the perfect environment for deliberate practice. Whether it's improving at work, learning a new hobby, or cultivating personal qualities like patience or resilience, the repetition inherent in daily life can be leveraged for growth. The key is to approach each day with a mindset of intentionality and a willingness to learn.

Overcoming Self-Centeredness: The Journey to Selflessness

At the heart of Phil's transformation is a shift from selfishness to selflessness. Initially, he uses the time loop for personal gain, manipulating others and indulging his desires. However, as he grows, he begins to focus on helping others—saving lives, performing acts of kindness, and making the world around him better.

This shift highlights a powerful lesson: true growth comes from moving beyond self-interest to contribute to the well-being of others. By using routine as an opportunity to practice selflessness, we can transform not only ourselves but also the lives of those around us.

Routine as a Path to Fulfillment

One of the film's most profound messages is that fulfillment often lies within the routines we take for granted. By embracing the repetitive nature of his existence, Phil discovers a deeper sense of purpose and joy. He learns to appreciate the small moments of beauty and connection that each day offers, transforming the ordinary into the extraordinary.

This lesson is particularly relevant in today's fast-paced, achievement-oriented culture. It reminds us that we don't need grand adventures or dramatic changes to find meaning. Instead, fulfillment can be found in the daily acts of living—showing kindness, pursuing growth, and savoring the present moment.

Practical Applications: How to Grow Through Routine

1. **Practice Mindfulness in Daily Activities:**
   Like Phil, we can find meaning in the smallest moments. Practicing mindfulness—being fully present during routine tasks—can help us appreciate the beauty and significance of everyday life.

2. **Set Intentional Goals Within Your Routine:**
   Identify areas for growth and use your daily routine as a framework for deliberate practice. Whether it's improving a skill, building a habit, or fostering relationships, approach each day with purpose.

3. **Focus on Connection:**
   Use routine interactions as opportunities to build emotional intelligence and deepen your relationships. Take the time to truly listen to and understand others.

4. **Embrace Challenges:**
   View repetitive challenges as opportunities to learn and grow. Like Phil, use setbacks as stepping stones to becoming a better version of yourself.

5. **Celebrate Small Wins:**
   Growth doesn't have to be dramatic. Celebrate the incremental progress you make through routine, recognizing that each step forward is meaningful.

Conclusion: Growth Through Routine

Phil Connors' journey in *Groundhog Day* is a testament to the transformative power of routine. His evolution from self-centered cynicism to compassionate self-awareness shows that even the most monotonous patterns of life hold the potential for growth and fulfillment. By embracing routine with intentionality and curiosity, we can unlock opportunities for self-improvement, connection, and meaning.

The lessons from Phil's story remind us that the key to growth isn't found in escaping the cycles of life but in engaging with them fully. By viewing routine not as a limitation but as a tool for transformation, we can turn every day into a stepping stone on the path to our best selves.

Chapter 3: Breaking Free from the Loop

Phil Connors' journey in *Groundhog Day* is not merely about enduring the repetitive cycle of a single day but about finding a way to break free from it. This process is deeply metaphorical, reflecting the human desire to escape patterns that feel confining or stagnant. Whether it is breaking free from bad habits, unfulfilling routines, or limiting mindsets, Phil's story offers profound insights into how we, too, can liberate ourselves from our own loops.

The Nature of the Loop: Recognizing Patterns in Life

Before we can break free from any loop, we must first recognize that we are in one. Loops in life are often subtle, manifesting as recurring frustrations, predictable failures, or repeated choices that lead to the same unsatisfactory outcomes. In Phil's case, the literal repetition of Groundhog Day forces him to confront the nature of his existence. For most of us, however, these loops are not as obvious.

Recognizing a loop requires self-awareness and reflection. Are there patterns in your life where the outcomes never seem to change? Perhaps it's a cycle of unhealthy relationships, a lack of progress in your career, or an inability to stick to personal goals. Acknowledging these patterns is the first step toward breaking free.

The Early Missteps: Escaping the Loop Without Growth

Phil's initial response to the time loop is to attempt escape without addressing the underlying issues in his life. He tries everything from hedonistic indulgence to outright suicide, but none of these actions provide the liberation he seeks. These missteps mirror the ways people often try to escape their own loops—by avoiding responsibility, blaming external circumstances, or seeking quick fixes.

Breaking free from a loop requires more than surface-level changes. It demands a deeper transformation, one that addresses the root causes of stagnation. For Phil, this meant confronting his selfishness, cynicism, and lack of connection to others. For us, it may involve examining our fears, limiting beliefs, or unhealthy behaviors.

Acceptance as the Key to Liberation

A pivotal moment in Phil's journey comes when he stops trying to escape the loop and begins to accept it. This acceptance is not a resignation to his fate but a recognition of the need to work within his circumstances rather than against them. He realizes that he cannot control the fact that he is reliving the same day, but he can control how he chooses to live it.

This shift in perspective is crucial for breaking free from any loop. Acceptance allows us to stop wasting energy on futile resistance and instead focus on the changes we can make. It is the foundation for growth and transformation.

Self-Improvement and Mastery: Turning Routine into Opportunity

One of the most inspiring aspects of Phil's story is how he uses the time loop to become a better person. Instead of seeing each repeated day as a punishment, he begins to view it as an opportunity. He learns new skills, helps others, and works to become the best version of himself.

This lesson applies directly to our own lives. Even when circumstances feel repetitive or limiting, we can use those conditions as a platform for self-improvement. By investing in our growth—whether through education, skill development, or personal reflection—we can transform routine into a pathway toward freedom.

Connecting with Others: The Role of Relationships in Breaking Free

A major turning point in Phil's journey is his growing empathy and connection with others. At the beginning of the film, he views the people of Punxsutawney as little more than props in the story of his life. Over time, he learns to see them as individuals with their own hopes, struggles, and humanity.

This shift highlights the importance of relationships in breaking free from personal loops. Isolation often perpetuates stagnation, while meaningful connections provide perspective, support, and motivation for change. By fostering empathy and building stronger relationships, we can break free from the self-centered patterns that keep us trapped.

The Power of Purpose: Finding Meaning in Repetition

Another critical element of Phil's transformation is his discovery of purpose. Initially, his actions are driven by self-interest or the hope of escaping the loop. As he grows, he begins to act out of a genuine desire to help others and make the most of his circumstances. This sense of purpose ultimately leads to his liberation.

Purpose is a powerful force for breaking free from life's loops. When we find meaning in our actions—whether through helping others, pursuing a passion, or striving for personal excellence—we create momentum that propels us forward. Purpose gives us the motivation to overcome challenges and the resilience to keep going, even when progress feels slow.

Letting Go of Control: The Final Step Toward Freedom

One of the film's most profound messages is that true freedom comes from letting go of the need to control everything. Phil's transformation is complete when he stops trying to manipulate the world around him and instead focuses on living each day fully and authentically.

Letting go of control doesn't mean giving up; it means recognizing the limits of our influence and focusing on what truly matters. This mindset shift is liberating because it allows us to embrace uncertainty and find peace in the present moment.

Practical Steps to Breaking Free from Your Own Loop

1. **Recognize the Loop:**
   Identify patterns in your life that feel repetitive or limiting. Reflect on the choices and behaviors that contribute to these cycles.

2. **Accept Your Circumstances:**
   Acknowledge the aspects of your situation that you cannot change and focus on what you can control. Acceptance is the foundation for growth.

3. **Invest in Self-Improvement:**
   Use repetition as an opportunity to refine your skills, deepen your knowledge, and become a better version of yourself.

4. **Foster Meaningful Connections:**
   Build relationships that inspire and support you. Empathy and connection are powerful tools for breaking out of self-centered patterns.

5. **Find Purpose:**
   Discover what gives your life meaning and let it guide your actions. Purpose creates momentum and helps you stay motivated.

6. **Let Go of the Need to Control Everything:**
   Focus on living authentically and embracing the present moment. Trust that growth and change will come naturally when you align your actions with your values.

Conclusion: The Path to Liberation

Phil Connors' journey in *Groundhog Day* is a powerful allegory for the process of breaking free from life's loops. It teaches us that liberation comes not from escape but from transformation—by embracing our circumstances, investing in growth, and finding meaning in the everyday.

Breaking free from the loop is not an instantaneous process. It requires patience, effort, and a willingness to look inward. But as Phil's story demonstrates, the rewards are worth it. By learning to live each day with purpose, connection, and authenticity, we can create a life that is not only free from repetition but rich with meaning and fulfillment.

Chapter 4: Finding Joy in Small Moments

One of the most enduring lessons from *Groundhog Day* is the value of finding joy in the small moments of life. At the heart of Phil Connors' transformation is his ability to shift his focus from grandiose ambitions to the subtle, often-overlooked beauty of everyday experiences. This chapter explores the profound impact of embracing life's simple pleasures and how doing so can enrich our lives, deepen our connections, and foster personal fulfillment.

The Trap of Seeking Happiness in Big Events

In modern society, happiness is often tied to major achievements or milestones: promotions, weddings, vacations, or significant purchases. We are conditioned to believe that joy lies in these grand moments, leaving us blind to the wealth of small, meaningful experiences that surround us every day.

At the start of *Groundhog Day*, Phil Connors embodies this mindset. He is dismissive of the quaint traditions of Punxsutawney, uninterested in the lives of the townspeople, and focused only on his career ambitions and personal gain. His dissatisfaction reflects the emptiness of a life that overlooks the small joys in pursuit of larger, often fleeting rewards.

The Power of Perspective: Rediscovering the Ordinary

Phil's transformation begins when he starts to notice and appreciate the ordinary moments of life. A sunrise over Punxsutawney, the warmth of a shared laugh, the satisfaction of helping someone in need—these small, seemingly inconsequential experiences take on profound significance as he relives the same day.

This shift in perspective is a key lesson for all of us. By slowing down and paying attention, we can uncover the beauty and joy hidden in everyday life. A cup of coffee on a quiet morning, a kind word from a stranger, or the sound of laughter from a loved one—these moments, while small, have the power to enrich our lives and bring a sense of peace and gratitude.

Practicing Gratitude: A Gateway to Joy

Gratitude is a powerful tool for finding joy in small moments. Phil's journey highlights this principle as he evolves from a man who takes everything for granted to someone who deeply appreciates the simple pleasures of life. Whether it's savoring a perfectly made pastry or taking time to help a neighbor, Phil learns to approach life with a sense of gratitude.

For us, cultivating gratitude begins with mindfulness—being present and attentive to the world around us. Simple practices like journaling about positive experiences, expressing thanks to others, or reflecting on the day's blessings can help shift our focus from what we lack to what we have. In doing so, we open ourselves to the joy inherent in life's smaller moments.

Connection Through Small Gestures

In *Groundhog Day*, Phil's newfound appreciation for small moments extends to his relationships with others. Instead of viewing the townspeople as background characters, he begins to see them as individuals worthy of his time and kindness. From catching a boy falling out of a tree to fixing an elderly man's car, Phil's acts of compassion stem from his awareness of the small ways he can make a difference.

This lesson reminds us of the power of small gestures in building connections and fostering joy. A smile, a kind word, or a small act of service can have a ripple effect, creating a sense of community and mutual appreciation. These moments of connection, though often fleeting, are among life's most meaningful experiences.

The Science of Savoring: Prolonging Joy

Psychologists have identified a concept called savoring—the act of fully experiencing and appreciating positive moments. Savoring involves slowing down, immersing yourself in the present, and consciously reflecting on the joy a moment brings. Phil's journey exemplifies this practice as he learns to savor the simple pleasures of life, from playing the piano to enjoying a quiet evening in the town square.

Savoring can be cultivated through intentional practices, such as:

1. **Mindful Awareness:**
   Focus fully on your senses during a positive experience. What do you see, hear, smell, taste, or feel?
2. **Sharing Joy:**
   Share your experiences with others, whether through conversation, storytelling, or shared activities.
3. **Gratitude Reflection:**
   Take time to reflect on the moment and express gratitude for it, either mentally or in a journal.
4. **Anticipation and Remembrance:**
   Prolong the joy of small moments by looking forward to them beforehand and reminiscing about them afterward.

By practicing savoring, we can deepen our appreciation of life's small joys and create lasting memories from even the simplest experiences.

The Role of Routine in Small Moments

Ironically, routines—often seen as boring or monotonous—are where small moments of joy often reside. The familiar rhythm of daily life creates opportunities to find beauty in repetition. In *Groundhog Day*, Phil discovers this truth as he transforms his daily routine into a series of meaningful acts, from perfecting his piano playing to learning everyone's name in town.

We can do the same in our own lives by approaching routine with curiosity and intentionality. Instead of rushing through daily tasks, we can pause to appreciate the small joys they offer, such as the aroma of freshly brewed coffee, the satisfaction of completing a task, or the comfort of familiar rituals.

Overcoming Obstacles to Joy

Finding joy in small moments requires overcoming common barriers, such as distraction, stress, and negative thinking. In Phil's case, his initial cynicism and self-centeredness prevent him from appreciating the world around him. His growth involves letting go of these obstacles and embracing a more open and optimistic outlook.

To overcome similar barriers in our own lives, we can:

1. **Limit Distractions:**
   Put away phones or devices during moments of connection or enjoyment to focus fully on the present.
2. **Manage Stress:**
   Incorporate stress-reducing practices like meditation, exercise, or deep breathing to create mental space for joy.
3. **Reframe Negativity:**
   Shift your perspective to focus on the positive aspects of a situation, even when challenges arise.

By addressing these obstacles, we can create the mental and emotional space needed to recognize and savor life's small joys.

Lessons from Phil: A New Outlook on Life

Phil Connors' journey teaches us that joy is not found in extraordinary events or achievements but in how we choose to experience the ordinary. By embracing the small moments, he transforms his repetitive existence into a life filled with meaning, connection, and fulfillment.

This lesson is universal. Regardless of our circumstances, we can choose to find joy in the simple pleasures that life offers. Whether it's the warmth of the sun on our skin, the sound of birdsong, or the kindness of a stranger, these small moments remind us of the beauty and wonder of being alive.

Practical Steps to Finding Joy in Small Moments

1. **Slow Down:**
   Take time to pause and be present, especially during routine activities.

2. **Practice Gratitude:**
   Reflect on the positive aspects of your day, no matter how small they may seem.

3. **Engage Your Senses:**
   Immerse yourself fully in the sensory details of your experiences.

4. **Celebrate the Mundane:**
   Find reasons to celebrate everyday achievements and rituals.

5. **Connect with Others:**
   Use small moments to build relationships and show kindness to those around you.

Conclusion: The Transformative Power of Small Moments

Finding joy in small moments is a skill, one that requires mindfulness, gratitude, and intentionality. Phil Connors' journey in *Groundhog Day* serves as a powerful reminder that life's greatest joys are often hidden in the ordinary. By learning to appreciate these moments, we can transform our routines into sources of fulfillment and create a life rich with meaning.

The ability to find joy in small moments is not just a lesson for those trapped in a time loop; it is a gift available to all of us, every single day.

Chapter 5: The *Groundhog Day* Philosophy for Life

The film *Groundhog Day* is not just a story about a weatherman trapped in a time loop; it is a timeless parable offering profound insights into how we can live better, more meaningful lives. At its core, the movie presents a philosophy for life that encompasses self-awareness, transformation, and the pursuit of purpose and fulfillment. This chapter explores the key principles of the *Groundhog Day* philosophy and how they can be applied to everyday living, helping us navigate life's challenges and opportunities with greater wisdom and clarity.

The Time Loop as a Metaphor for Life

In *Groundhog Day*, Phil Connors relives February 2nd over and over again. This endless repetition is a powerful metaphor for the routines and patterns that define much of human existence. While most of us are not literally trapped in a time loop, we often feel stuck in cycles of behavior, thought, and circumstance.

The *Groundhog Day* philosophy encourages us to see these cycles not as limitations but as opportunities for growth. By embracing the repetition in our lives, we can use it as a platform for self-improvement and deeper understanding. Instead of viewing each day as a chore, we can approach it as a new chance to refine our actions, deepen our connections, and align ourselves with our values.

Principle 1: Acceptance as the Foundation of Change

Phil's transformation begins with acceptance. Initially, he resists the time loop, trying to escape or manipulate it to no avail. It is only when he accepts his circumstances that he begins to find meaning and purpose in his situation.

This principle applies to life outside the time loop. Acceptance does not mean resignation or passivity; it means acknowledging the reality of our circumstances and choosing to work within them. Whether it's a challenging job, a difficult relationship, or an unchangeable past, acceptance is the first step toward meaningful change. By letting go of resistance, we free up energy to focus on what we can control.

Principle 2: The Power of Intentionality

One of the most striking aspects of Phil's transformation is his shift from aimlessness to intentionality. In the early stages of the time loop, he acts impulsively, indulging in hedonistic pleasures and selfish pursuits. Over time, he begins to live each day with purpose, setting goals for himself and taking deliberate actions to achieve them.

The *Groundhog Day* philosophy teaches us the importance of intentional living. Each day is an opportunity to make choices that align with our values and aspirations. By setting clear intentions—whether it's to learn a new skill, help someone in need, or simply be kinder to ourselves—we can create a life filled with purpose and fulfillment.

Principle 3: Growth Through Repetition

Repetition is often seen as monotonous, but *Groundhog Day* reframes it as a powerful tool for growth. Phil uses the time loop to practice and master new skills, deepen his understanding of others, and refine his character.

This principle reminds us that repetition is not inherently negative. It is through repeated effort that we learn, improve, and achieve mastery. Whether it's practicing an instrument, honing a craft, or building a healthy habit, growth comes from consistent, intentional effort over time. The key is to approach repetition with curiosity and a commitment to learning.

Principle 4: The Importance of Connection

At the start of the film, Phil is isolated, cynical, and dismissive of others. As he relives the same day, he begins to see the people around him as individuals with their own stories, struggles, and joys. This shift allows him to build genuine connections and find fulfillment in acts of kindness and service.

The *Groundhog Day* philosophy emphasizes the value of relationships. True happiness and meaning come not from what we achieve for ourselves but from the connections we build with others. By cultivating empathy, practicing active listening, and showing kindness, we can create a life rich with meaningful relationships.

Principle 5: Finding Meaning in the Present Moment

One of the film's most profound lessons is the importance of living in the present. Initially, Phil is preoccupied with escaping the time loop or manipulating it for personal gain. As he grows, he learns to savor the moment—to find joy in a sunrise, a conversation, or a simple act of kindness.

This principle aligns with mindfulness practices, which encourage us to focus on the here and now rather than dwelling on the past or worrying about the future. By being fully present, we can experience life more deeply and find meaning in even the smallest moments.

Principle 6: The Journey to Selflessness

Phil's journey is ultimately a shift from selfishness to selflessness. At the start of the film, his actions are driven by personal gain. Over time, he begins to act out of genuine care for others, helping the townspeople and contributing to the community.

The *Groundhog Day* philosophy teaches us that true fulfillment comes from giving, not taking. By focusing on how we can serve and uplift others, we create a ripple effect of positivity that enhances our own lives as well as those around us.

Applying the *Groundhog Day* Philosophy to Everyday Life

The principles of the *Groundhog Day* philosophy are not limited to the confines of a time loop. They offer practical guidance for living a more intentional, connected, and fulfilling life. Here are some actionable steps:

1. **Embrace Routine as an Opportunity for Growth:**
   View your daily routines as chances to refine your actions and develop new skills.
2. **Set Clear Intentions:**
   Approach each day with a specific goal or purpose in mind, no matter how small.
3. **Practice Gratitude:**
   Reflect on the positive aspects of your life and express thanks for the small joys and blessings.
4. **Cultivate Empathy:**
   Take the time to understand and connect with others, recognizing their humanity and individuality.
5. **Live in the Present:**
   Focus on the here and now, savoring the experiences and opportunities each moment offers.
6. **Serve Others:**
   Look for ways to contribute to the well-being of those around you, whether through small acts of kindness or larger efforts to make a difference.

Conclusion: A Philosophy for a Meaningful Life

The *Groundhog Day* philosophy is a powerful framework for living a richer, more purposeful life. By embracing its principles—acceptance, intentionality, growth, connection, mindfulness, and selflessness—we can break free from the cycles that hold us back and create a life filled with meaning and joy.

Phil Connors' journey is a reminder that transformation is always possible, even in the face of monotony or challenge. Each day, no matter how repetitive or ordinary, holds the potential for growth, connection, and discovery. By approaching life with the mindset embodied in *Groundhog Day*, we can unlock the profound beauty of our existence and live in alignment with our highest values.

Appendix A: Personal Growth Exercises

The journey of personal growth is a lifelong process that requires intentional effort, self-reflection, and a willingness to embrace change. Drawing inspiration from the lessons of *Groundhog Day*, this appendix provides a collection of practical exercises designed to help you cultivate self-awareness, build meaningful habits, and unlock your potential. These exercises are flexible and can be adapted to suit your unique circumstances and goals.

1. Daily Reflection Journal

Objective: Cultivate self-awareness and track progress over time.

How to Do It:

- Set aside 10–15 minutes at the end of each day to reflect on your experiences.
- Use a journal to answer the following questions:
  1. What went well today?
  2. What challenges did I face, and how did I handle them?
  3. What did I learn about myself today?
  4. What am I grateful for?
- Over time, review your entries to identify patterns, areas for growth, and accomplishments.

Benefit: Encourages mindfulness, fosters gratitude, and helps you gain clarity about your strengths and areas for improvement.

2. The Habit Tracker

Objective: Build consistency in positive habits and break negative ones.

How to Do It:

- Create a list of habits you want to build (e.g., exercising, meditating, reading) or break (e.g., excessive screen time, procrastination).
- Use a habit tracker app or a simple chart to mark each day you successfully follow through.
- Start small: Focus on 1–3 habits at a time to avoid overwhelm.
- Celebrate small wins, and don't get discouraged by setbacks.

Benefit: Reinforces good behaviors through positive reinforcement and creates a sense of achievement.

3. The Gratitude Practice

Objective: Develop a positive outlook and appreciate the small joys in life.

How to Do It:

- Each morning or evening, write down three things you are grateful for.
- Be specific. For example, instead of "I'm grateful for my family," write, "I'm grateful for the conversation I had with my sister today."
- Reflect on why these things matter to you.

Benefit: Shifts focus from what's lacking to what's present, fostering a mindset of abundance and contentment.

4. The 1% Better Rule
Objective: Focus on incremental improvement over time.
How to Do It:

- Identify one area of your life you want to improve (e.g., health, career, relationships).
- Set a small, achievable goal for daily improvement—just 1% better than the day before. For example:
    - Health: Add one more glass of water to your daily intake.
    - Career: Spend 10 minutes networking or learning a new skill.
    - Relationships: Send a thoughtful text or make a phone call to someone you care about.
- Track your progress and adjust as needed.

Benefit: Breaks down big goals into manageable steps, making growth sustainable and less overwhelming.

5. Mindful Moments Exercise
Objective: Cultivate mindfulness and presence in daily life.
How to Do It:

- Choose a specific activity you do daily, such as brushing your teeth, drinking coffee, or walking.
- During this activity, focus entirely on the present moment. Notice the sensations, sounds, smells, and feelings without judgment.
- If your mind wanders, gently bring it back to the present.

Benefit: Enhances awareness, reduces stress, and helps you savor life's small pleasures.

6. Acts of Kindness Challenge
Objective: Strengthen your sense of connection and compassion.
How to Do It:

- Set a goal to perform one small act of kindness each day. Examples include:
    - Complimenting a coworker.
    - Paying for someone's coffee.
    - Helping a neighbor with a task.
    - Writing a thank-you note.
- Keep a log of your acts of kindness to reflect on the impact they've had on others and yourself.

Benefit: Builds empathy, strengthens relationships, and fosters a sense of purpose.

7. The "Ideal Day" Visualization
Objective: Clarify your values and align your actions with your ideal life.
How to Do It:

- Sit in a quiet place and close your eyes. Imagine your ideal day, starting from the moment you wake up to the time you go to bed.
- Visualize specific details: Where are you? Who are you with? What are you doing? How do you feel?
- Write down your vision and compare it to your current reality. Identify one or two changes you can make to bring your current life closer to your ideal day.

Benefit: Provides a clear sense of direction and motivation to align your actions with your values and goals.

8. The "Wheel of Life" Assessment

Objective: Evaluate your life balance and identify areas for growth.

How to Do It:

- Draw a circle and divide it into 8–10 sections, each representing a key area of your life (e.g., health, career, relationships, personal growth, finances, recreation, spirituality).
- Rate your satisfaction in each area on a scale from 1 to 10, with 1 being dissatisfied and 10 being highly satisfied.
- Reflect on the results. What areas need more attention? What areas are thriving?
- Set one goal for improvement in an area where your satisfaction is low.

Benefit: Offers a holistic view of your life and helps prioritize areas for growth.

9. The "Stop, Start, Continue" Framework

Objective: Identify behaviors to change or maintain for personal growth.

How to Do It:

- Create three columns labeled "Stop," "Start," and "Continue."
- Reflect on your habits and actions:
    - **Stop:** What is holding you back or draining your energy?
    - **Start:** What new behaviors or habits could benefit you?
    - **Continue:** What is working well and should be maintained?
- Commit to implementing these changes over the next month.

Benefit: Encourages intentional decision-making and helps eliminate unproductive habits.

10. The Weekly Review
Objective: Regularly assess progress and adjust your approach.
How to Do It:

- Set aside 30–60 minutes each week to review your goals and reflect on the past week.
- Answer the following questions:
  1. What did I accomplish this week?
  2. What challenges did I face, and how did I address them?
  3. What could I improve next week?
  4. What am I looking forward to in the coming week?
- Adjust your plans and priorities based on your reflections.

Benefit: Provides a structured approach to self-improvement and keeps you accountable to your goals.

Conclusion

Personal growth is not about dramatic overnight transformations but about consistent, intentional actions taken over time. The exercises in this appendix are designed to help you cultivate a growth mindset, embrace the lessons of *Groundhog Day*, and create a life of meaning and fulfillment. Whether you choose one exercise or integrate several into your routine, remember that growth is a journey, and every small step forward brings you closer to your best self.

Message from the Author:

I hope you enjoyed this book, I love astrology and knew there was not a book such as this out on the shelf. I love metaphysical items as well. Please check out my other books:

-Life of Government Benefits

-My life of Hell

-My life with Hydrocephalus

-Red Sky

-World Domination:Woman's rule

-World Domination:Woman's Rule 2: The War

-Life and Banishment of Apophis: book 1

-The Kidney Friendly Diet

-The Ultimate Hemp Cookbook

-Creating a Dispensary(legally)

-Cleanliness throughout life: the importance of showering from childhood to adulthood.

-Strong Roots: The Risks of Overcoddling children

-Hemp Horoscopes: Cosmic Insights and Earthly Healing

- Celestial Hemp Navigating the Zodiac: Through the Green Cosmos

-Astrological Hemp: Aligning The Stars with Earth's Ancient Herb

-The Astrological Guide to Hemp: Stars, Signs, and Sacred Leaves

-Green Growth: Innovative Marketing Strategies for your Hemp Products and Dispensary

-Cosmic Cannabis

-Astrological Munchies

-Henry The Hemp

-Zodiacal Roots: The Astrological Soul Of Hemp

- Green Constellations: Intersection of Hemp and Zodiac

-Hemp in The Houses: An astrological Adventure Through The Cannabis Galaxy

-Galactic Ganja Guide
Heavenly Hemp
Zodiac Leaves
Doctor Who Astrology
Cannastrology
Stellar Satvias and Cosmic Indicas
<u>Celestial Cannabis: A Zodiac Journey</u>
AstroHerbology: The Sky and The Soil: Volume 1
AstroHerbology:Celestial Cannabis:Volume 2
Cosmic Cannabis Cultivation
The Starry Guide to Herbal Harmony: Volume 1
The Starry Guide to Herbal Harmony: Cannabis Universe: Volume
2
Yugioh Astrology: Astrological Guide to Deck, Duels and more
Nightmare Mansion: Echoes of The Abyss
Nightmare Mansion 2: Legacy of Shadows
Nightmare Mansion 3: Shadows of the Forgotten
Nightmare Mansion 4: Echoes of the Damned
The Life and Banishment of Apophis: Book 2
Nightmare Mansion: Halls of Despair
<u>Healing with Herb: Cannabis and Hydrocephalus</u>
<u>Planetary Pot: Aligning with Astrological Herbs: Volume 1</u>
Fast Track to Freedom: 30 Days to Financial Independence Using AI, Assets, and Agile Hustles
<u>Cosmic Hemp Pathways</u>
How to Become Financially Free in 30 Days: 10,000 Paths to Prosperity
Zodiacal Herbage: Astrological Insights: Volume 1
Nightmare Mansion: Whispers in the Walls
The Daleks Invade Atlantis
Henry the hemp and Hydrocephalus

10X The Kidney Friendly Diet
Cannabis Universe: Adult coloring book
Hemp Astrology: The Healing Power of the Stars
Zodiacal Herbage: Astrological Insights: Cannabis Universe: Volume 2
<u>**Planetary Pot: Aligning with Astrological Herbs: Cannabis Universes: Volume 2**</u>
Doctor Who Meets the Replicators and SG-1: The Ultimate Battle for Survival
Nightmare Mansion: Curse of the Blood Moon
<u>**The Celestial Stoner: A Guide to the Zodiac**</u>
Cosmic Pleasures: Sex Toy Astrology for Every Sign
Hydrocephalus Astrology: Navigating the Stars and Healing Waters
Lapis and the Mischievous Chocolate Bar

Celestial Positions: Sexual Astrology for Every Sign
Apophis's Shadow Work Journal: : A Journey of Self-Discovery and Healing
Kinky Cosmos: Sexual Kink Astrology for Every Sign
Digital Cosmos: The Astrological Digimon Compendium
Stellar Seeds: The Cosmic Guide to Growing with Astrology
Apophis's Daily Gratitude Journal

Cat Astrology: Feline Mysteries of the Cosmos
The Cosmic Kama Sutra: An Astrological Guide to Sexual Positions
Unleash Your Potential: A Guided Journal Powered by AI Insights
Whispers of the Enchanted Grove

Cosmic Pleasures: An Astrological Guide to Sexual Kinks
369, 12 Manifestation Journal

Whisper of the nocturne journal(blank journal for writing or drawing)

The Boogey Book

Locked In Reflection: A Chastity Journey Through Locktober

Generating Wealth Quickly:

How to Generate $100,000 in 24 Hours

Star Magic: Harness the Power of the Universe

The Flatulence Chronicles: A Fart Journal for Self-Discovery

The Doctor and The Death Moth

Seize the Day: A Personal Seizure Tracking Journal

The Ultimate Boogeyman Safari: A Journey into the Boogie World and Beyond

Whispers of Samhain: 1,000 Spells of Love, Luck, and Lunar Magic: Samhain Spell Book

Apophis's guides:

Witch's Spellbook Crafting Guide for Halloween

<u>Frost & Flame: The Enchanted Yule Grimoire of 1000 Winter Spells</u>

<u>The Ultimate Boogey Goo Guide & Spooky Activities for Halloween Fun</u>

Harmony of the Scales: A Libra's Spellcraft for Balance and Beauty

The Enchanted Advent: 36 Days of Christmas Wonders

Nightmare Mansion: The Labyrinth of Screams

Harvest of Enchantment: 1,000 Spells of Gratitude, Love, and Fortune for Thanksgiving

The Boogey Chronicles: A Journal of Nightly Encounters and Shadowy Secrets

The 12 Days of Financial Freedom: A Step-by-Step Christmas Countdown to Transform Your Finances

Sigil of the Eternal Spiral Blank Journal

A Christmas Feast: Timeless Recipes for Every Meal

Cosmic Sales: The Astrological Guide to Black Friday Shopping

Legends of the Corn Mother and Other Harvest Myths

Whispers of the Harvest: The Corn Mother's Journal

The Evergreen Spellbook

The Doctor Meets the Boogeyman

The White Witch of Rose Hall's SpellBook

The Gingerbread Golem's Shadow: A Study in Sweet Darkness

The Gingerbread Golem Codex: An Academic Exploration of Sweet Myths

The Gingerbread Golem Grimoire: Sweet Magicks and Spells for the Festive Witch

The Curse of the Gingerbread Golem

10-minute Christmas Crafts for kids

<u>Christmas Crisis Solutions: The Ultimate Last-Minute Survival Guide</u>

Gingerbread Golem Recipes: Holiday Treats with a Magical Twist

The Infinite Key: Unlocking Mystical Secrets of the Ages

Enchanted Yule: A Wiccan and Pagan Guide to a Magical and Memorable Season

Dinosaurs of Power: Unlocking Ancient Magick

Astro-Dinos: The Cosmic Guide to Prehistoric Wisdom

Gallifrey's Yule Logs: A Festive Doctor Who Cookbook

The Dino Grimoire: Secrets of Prehistoric Magick

The Gift They Never Knew They Needed

The Gingerbread Golem's Culinary Alchemy: Enchanting Recipes for a Sweetly Dark Feast

A Time Lord Christmas: Holiday Adventures with the Doctor

Krampusproofing Your Home: Defensive Strategies for Yule

Silent Frights: A Collection of Christmas Creepypastas to Chill Your Bones

Santa Raptor's Jolly Carnage: A Dino-Claus Christmas Tale

Prehistoric Palettes: A Dino Wicca Coloring Journey

The Christmas Wishkeeper Chronicles

The Starlight Sleigh: A Holiday Journey

Elf Secrets: The True Magic of the North Pole

Candy Cane Conjurations

Cooking with Kids: Recipes Under 20 Minutes

Doctor Who: The TARDIS Confiscation

The Anxiety First Aid Kit: Quick Tools to Calm Your Mind

Frosty Whispers: A Winter's Tale

The Infinite Key: Unlocking the Secrets to Prosperity, Resilience, and Purpose

The Grasping Void: Why You'll Regret This Purchase

Astrology for Busy Bees: Star Signs Simplified

The Instant Focus Formula: Cut Through the Noise

The Secret Language of Colors: Unlocking the Emotional Codes

Sacred Fossil Chronicles: Blank Journal

The Christmas Cottage Miracle

Feeding Frenzy: Graboid-Inspired Recipes

Manifest in Minutes: The Quick Law of Attraction Guide

The Symbiote Chronicles: Doctor Who's Venomous Journey

Think Tiny, Grow Big: The Minimalist Mindset

The Energy Key: Unlocking Limitless Motivation

New Year, New Magic: Manifesting Your Best Year Yet

Unstoppable You: Mastering Confidence in Minutes

Infinite Energy: The Secret to Never Feeling Drained

Lightning Focus: Mastering the Art of Productivity in a Distracted World

Saturnalia Manifestation Magick: A Guide to Unlocking Abundance During the Solstice

Graboids and Garland: The Ultimate Tremors-Themed Christmas Guide

12 Nights of Holiday Magic

The Power of Pause: 60-Second Mindfulness Practices

The Quick Reset: How to Reclaim Your Life After Burnout

The Shadow Eater: A Tale of Despair and Survival

The Micro-Mastery Method: Transform Your Skills in Just Minutes a Day

Reclaiming Time: How to Live More by Doing Less

Chronovore: The Eternal Nexus

The Mind Reset: Unlocking Your Inner Peace in a Chaotic World

Confidence Code: Building Unshakable Self-Belief

Baby the Vampire Terrier

Baby the Vampire Terrier's Christmas Adventure

Celestial Streams: The Content Creator's Astrology Manual

The Wealth Whisperer: Unlocking Abundance with Everyday Actions

The Energy Equation: Maximize Your Output Without Burning Out

The Happiness Algorithm: Science-Backed Steps to Joyful Living

Stress-Free Success: Achieving Goals Without Anxiety

Mindful Wealth: The New Blueprint for Financial Freedom

The Festive Flavors of New Year: A Culinary Celebration

The Master's Gambit: Keys of Eternal Power

Shadowed Secrets: Groundhog Day Mysteries

Beneath the Burrow: Lessons from the Groundhog

Spring's Whispers: The Groundhog's Prediction

The Limitless Mindset: Unlock Your Untapped Potential

The Focus Funnel: How to Cut Through Chaos and Get Results

Bold Moves: Building Courage to Live on Your Terms

The Daily Shift: Simple Practices for Lasting Transformation

The Quarter-Life Reset: Thriving in Your 20s and 30s

The Art of Shadowplay: Building Your Own Personal Myth

If you want solar for your home go here: https://www.harborsolar.live/apophisenterprises/

Get Some Tarot cards: https://www.makeplayingcards.com/sell/ apophis-occult-shop

<u>**Get some shirts: https://www.bonfire.com/store/apophis-shirt-emporium/**</u>

<u>Instagrams:</u>
@apophis_enterprises,
@apophisbookemporium,
@apophisscardshop
Twitter: @apophisenterpr1
 Tiktok:@apophisenterprise
Youtube: @sg1fan23477, @FiresideRetreatKingdom
Hive: @sg1fan23477
CheeLee: @SG1fan23477

Podcast: Apophis Chat Zone: https://open.spotify.com/show/
5zXbrCLEV2xzCp8ybrfHsk?si=fb4d4fdbdce44dec

Newsletter: https://apophiss-newsletter-27c897.beehiiv.com/

If you want to support me or see posts of other projects that I have come over to: **buymeacoffee.com/mpetchinskg**
I post there daily several times a day

Get your Dinowicca or Christmas themed digital products, especially Santa Raptor songs and other musics. Here:
https://sg1fan23477.gumroad.com

Apophis Yuletide Digital has not only digital Christmas items, but it will have all things with Dinowicca as well as other Digital products.